Contents

About hockey

Hockey is a stick and ball game played by two teams of 11 players (and two substitutes) on either an indoor or outdoor field. Players propel the ball with the stick towards their goal. The aim of the game is to score goals by sending the ball between the goal posts.

Younger players (aged seven years and under) play a modified version of the game, called minkey. Minkey is played on a smaller field, and there is no driving or hitting allowed.

Play is controlled by an umpire, who also begins play and decides when a goal is scored and when infringements of the rules occur. Two umpires control senior matches, while one controls a junior match. A junior match is played over two 30-minute halves, with a five-minute half-time break. A senior match consists of two 35-minute halves with a five-minute half-time break.

The coach assigns each player a position on the field. The modern game demands that players defend as well as attack so being able to move up and down the field quickly is important.

Hockey has been one of the sports played at the Olympic Games since 1908. However, it was only recently – 1984 – that women's hockey was first played at the Olympic Games. It is a very popular sport in Australia, the Netherlands, Germany, Great Britain, India and Pakistan.

UK highlights

Participation

Hockey's appeal is widespread. 3.57 million young people aged between four and 18 play regularly, making hockey one of the top ten participation sports in the UK. More than 2.5 million adults – evenly divided between men and women – also play regularly. There are 1,615 clubs operating throughout the UK with 4,559 teams registered with English Hockey.

The English Hockey Network provides support at all levels of the sport. Development managers and assistants, based at ten centres across the country, can help clubs, schools and counties with coaching, umpiring, talent identification and facility development.

Jackie Empson (left) has represented England at U16, U18, U21 and at senior level.

Bill Waugh first played hockey at the age of 11 at school. He has been the captain of England at U16, U18 and U21 levels. Now aged 25, he is captain of England's senior team.

The English Hockey Association was formed in June 1997, when the All England Women's Hockey Association combined with the Men's Hockey Association and the Mixed Hockey Association to become the new governing body of the sport. In recent years support from outside agencies – particularly the English Sports Council – has enabled the sport to complement its voluntary structure with expertise from professional coaches, youth development and marketing.

Competitions

Nationally there is a highly organised competitive structure, with leagues operating from the elite English Hockey League (EHL) right down to local leagues. Teams that finish in the top four of the EHL Premier League go forward to a play-off tournament, held during the first May Bank Holiday weekend each year at the National Hockey Stadium in Milton Keynes.

The winners of both the Men's and Women's Champion Leagues then go through to the European Championships. In 1999 the Men's European Championships will be held in Padua, Italy, and the Women's in Cologne, Germany. Great Britain will be represented by teams from Ireland, Wales, Scotland and England. The winners, or best performing sides, will be chosen to represent Great Britain in the next Olympics.

History of hockey

Hockey dates back to ancient times. The earliest pictorial representation of the game was a relief discovered in Athens in 1922 as workers were repairing the ancient wall in a building of the Greek leader Thermistocles. The relief, or impression, dates back 2500 years, and shows two players holding curved sticks above a ball.

Hurling

The most likely ancestor of the modern game of hockey is hurling, but it is also closely related to two games that are still played today. These are shinty, a Scottish game, and bandy, a game played in both England and Wales.

Hurling is the national game of the Irish. While its exact origins are unknown, it appears in many Irish legends, one of which tells of a lethal hurling match (with nine hurlers on each team) in which the defeated team lost not only the game – but their lives.

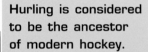

Hurling is considered to be the ancestor of modern hockey.

A hockey match on an English beach in 1905

An English game

Hurling crossed the sea from Ireland to England and became known as hockey. One of the first organised hockey clubs in England – the Blackheath Rugby and Hockey Club – was formed in 1840. The game was very rough, but a refinement to the rules in 1874 prohibited raising of the stick.

The rules of the game, which were standardised by the Wimbledon Hockey Club in 1883, were adopted by the English Hockey Association in 1886.

The first international hockey match was played between England and Ireland in 1895, with Ireland winning. Hockey was first included at the Olympic Games in 1908, and England won.

An international sport

In 1924, the Federation Internationale de Hockey (FIH) was formed with 47 countries as members. Hockey is now played in many countries, including Australia, the Netherlands, Germany, Great Britain, India, Pakistan, China, Canada, Spain and Korea.

At the international competition level, teams compete in the Olympic Games, the World Cup and the Champions Trophy Tournament.

What you need to play

The pitch

Hockey is played on a rectangular field called a pitch, 90 metres long and 55 metres wide. For a junior match, the pitch may be reduced to 45 metres long and 27 metres wide, depending on the age of the players. Note that the 25-metre lines actually measure 23 metres (25 yards) from the back line to the sideline.

The hockey stick

Your hockey stick should weigh between 340 and 794 grams (light to medium weight), and be just under hip height. It must be comfortable to grip and easy to manoeuvre. The head of the stick has a large curve to make ball handling simpler. The handle surface will allow a non-slip grip.

The pitch

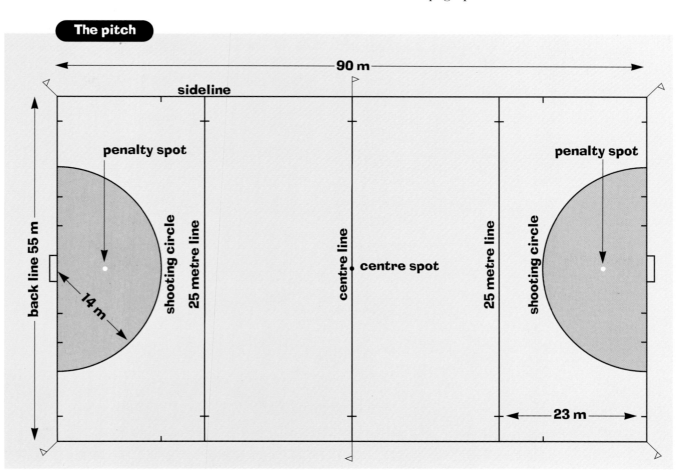

At club level, players wear a numbered shirt, shorts or a skirt, shoes and socks in team colours. Your shoes should be suitable for the playing surface. If playing indoors, trainers with short grips are best. Boots with moulded studs are best on grass.

The goalkeeper's equipment

The ball

The ball for practice or play is usually white and weighs between 155 and 163 grams. It has a circumference of between 220 and 230 millimetres and is without seams.

Protective equipment

Two pieces of protective equipment are essential. First, to protect the legs, players wear shin guards made from dense foam and/or rubber, which are comfortable and non-restrictive. Secondly, all players should wear a specially moulded mouthguard to protect their teeth.

Because the goalkeeper faces high-speed goal shots, he or she must wear protective equipment, including a helmet with visor, throat protector, chest pads, shoulder pads, elbow pads, box, thigh pads, leg and knee guards, gloves and padded boots or 'kickers'.

Rules

Start of play

Before play starts, the coach assigns each player a position on the field. To begin play, the captains of both teams toss to decide who will take first possession of the ball. Then, the game starts with a **centre pass**, which is also used to restart play after a goal or half-time. The centre pass is taken from the middle of the centre line, and all players must be in their defensive half and five metres or more from the ball.

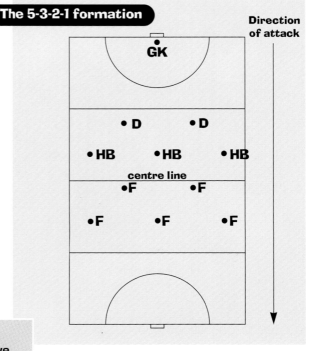

This is an attacking formation, to be used whenever your team has the ball. There are five forwards (F), three half backs (HB), two defenders (D) and one goalkeeper (GK).

Players' positions

Players must defend as well as attack because the pitch is divided into an attacking half and a defending half. When the ball is in your attacking half, your aim is to advance it towards your goal, and then to score. When your opponent has the ball, your aim is to limit your opponents' progress towards goal, and you may even steal the ball from them.

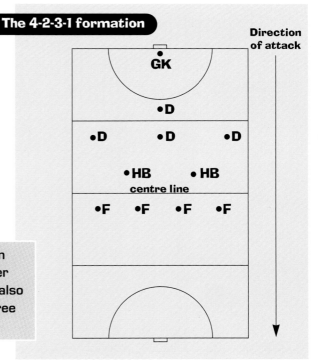

This is a defending formation, to be used when the opposing team has the ball. The goalkeeper (GK) is assisted by a defender (D). There are also four forwards (F), two half backs (HB) and three more defenders (D).

The role of the goalkeeper

The goalkeeper's job is to save goals. While free to move outside the shooting circle, the goalie loses certain privileges when doing so. These privileges are:

• being allowed to kick the ball within the shooting circle;

• stopping the oncoming airborne ball with their hand, then clearing it when it drops to the ground; and

• blocking a shot with any part of the body.

Continuing play

The team scoring the most goals wins, so the aim of the game is to score goals. After the centre pass, players try to get possession of the ball to advance it towards their goal. A goal is scored when the ball passes between the vertical posts and under the cross bar. You can only score from inside the shooting circle. The non-scoring team takes possession after a goal is scored.

Ball out of play

The ball is out of play when it passes over the sideline or goal-line. When it passes over the sideline, a **hit-in** is taken by the non-offending team from where

the ball crossed the line. All players must be at least five metres from the ball.

When the ball crosses the goal-line, play is re-started by:

• a corner hit, which is awarded when a defender unintentionally sends the ball over their goal-line within the 25-metre line;

• a 16-metre hit, which is awarded to the defender when an attacker sends the ball over the goal-line; or

• a **penalty corner**, which is awarded when a defender intentionally sends the ball over their goal-line.

Rules

Fouls

Stick offences

These types of foul relate to use of the stick. The first is known as 'back of stick'. You may only play the ball legally from the flat side of the stick. Accidental contact with the back of the stick is not usually penalised.

The second is known as 'stick check'. At no time are you allowed to strike, hit, hook, hold or generally interfere with an opponent's stick.

The third is known as 'dangerous play'. It is a foul to hit the ball so it rises dangerously, and a player who hits wildly at any height into an opponent will also be penalised. However, a controlled flick or **scoop** is legal.

Careful!

As a general rule, don't swing wildly at the ball on the backswing or follow through. Never raise your stick so that it endangers another player.

Stick check

You commit a foul if you interfere with another player's stick. A free hit will be awarded.

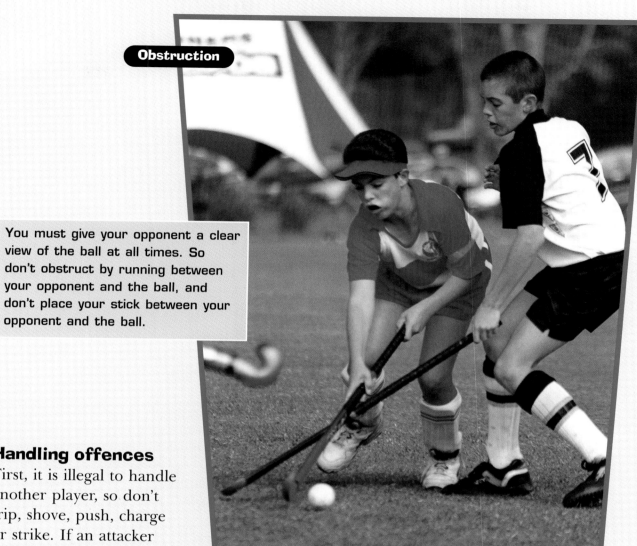

Obstruction

You must give your opponent a clear view of the ball at all times. So don't obstruct by running between your opponent and the ball, and don't place your stick between your opponent and the ball.

Handling offences

First, it is illegal to handle another player, so don't trip, shove, push, charge or strike. If an attacker over-runs the ball, then gets pushed from behind by a defender, the defender has committed a foul by handling an attacker. While defending, if you attempt to force your opponent away from the ball by charging with your shoulder and/or arm, you will also be fouled.

Secondly, the ball may only be moved with the stick so don't stop the ball with your hand. But if you raise your hand to protect yourself from a raised ball, you will not be penalised.

Thirdly, play on is usually called if the ball accidentally hits your foot. But if you use your foot deliberately to stop or

propel the ball, a foul is called. Always bend low, keeping your stick grounded to prevent this foul.

Free hits

When an opponent infringes the rules, a **free hit** is awarded, which is taken where the breach occurred. No player may be within five metres of this spot. The ball may be pushed or driven, but not scooped.

Free hits may be awarded all over the field except in the goal circles, which results in a penalty corner.

Rules

Penalties

The umpire may award penalties, which are different from free hits. There are two types awarded: penalty corner and penalty stroke.

Penalty corner

Your opponents will receive a penalty corner if you accidentally infringe in the goal circle or deliberately infringe in the 25-metre area. The most common infringements resulting in a penalty corner are dangerous play, **obstruction** or kicking the ball.

Penalty stroke

The umpire will award a **penalty stroke** when a defender intentionally breaches the rules in the shooting circle or when an accidental foul prevents an otherwise probable goal. The penalty stroke is taken from the penalty spot seven metres in front of the goal. The striker may take one step and flick, scoop or push the ball at any height toward the goal.

Five defenders stand behind the goal-line and the remaining six players must stand in their half. The attackers line up around the goal circle, and the ball is then hit into play from the goal-line by an attacker 10 metres from the goal. An attacker must first stop the ball, then try to score a goal.

Penalty corner

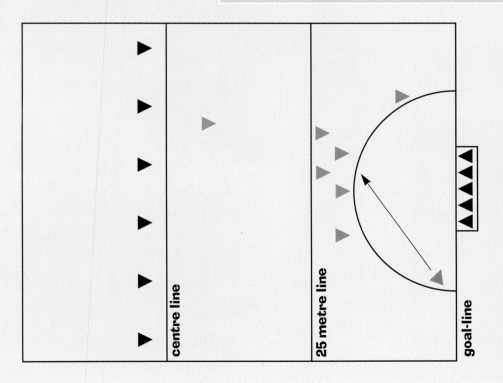

centre line

25 metre line

goal-line

Skills

Gripping the stick

The standard grip

The grip is the same for both right- and left-handers, and is used for every hockey skill, except the drive.

Place your left hand at the top of the stick so that your thumb and forefinger form a 'V' down the back of the stick. Now place your right hand about one-third to halfway down the shaft of the stick. Some players may prefer to point the index finger of this lower hand down the shaft.

Standard grip

Reverse grip

Use your lower hand to provide support and control.

Reversing the stick

As the ball can only be played from the flat surface of the stick, you must learn to turn or **reverse** the stick when the ball is to be played on the reverse side.

Rotate the stick one half-turn by loosening the lower hand and rotating the upper hand. The loosened lower hand provides support and control as the stick is rotated, and the lower grip is tightened once the stick is in the reverse position.

Skills

Dribbling the ball

Dribbling is the skill of propelling the ball with the stick while running. Aim to keep the ball within easy reach so you can quickly stop or change direction. Remember that passing the ball to a team-mate in a better position, rather than trying to get into that position by dribbling, works better.

Scanning is the skill of looking around to spot your options, and is important for dribbling.

As you scan, consider:

• where is the most space?

• will I pass or keep the ball?

• where are my team-mates moving to?

• will I advance left or right, forwards or backwards?

The open dribble

The **open dribble** is used when you want to advance quickly down the open field, while keeping control of the ball and without an opponent challenging you.

With the standard grip, bend forward and tap the ball along to your right and in front of you.

The close dribble

Use the **close dribble** when trying to pass an opponent. Keep the ball close to the stick, but at about 30 to 40 centimetres from your feet.

Open dribble

Have the ball in control by keeping it close to your stick.

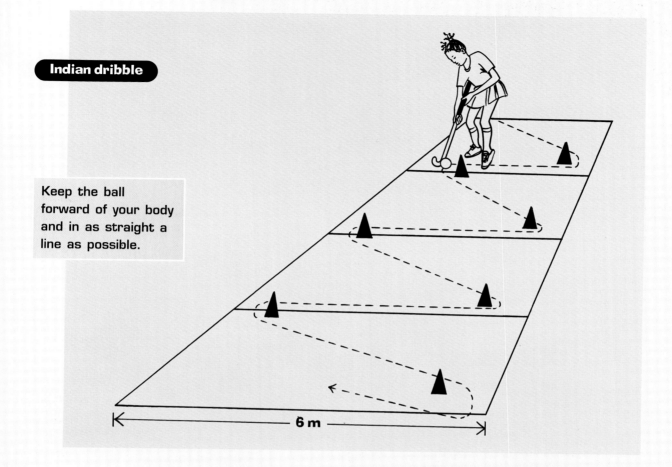

Indian dribble

Keep the ball forward of your body and in as straight a line as possible.

6 m

The Indian dribble

The **Indian dribble** is used to dribble around opponents. It allows the dribbler the opportunity to pass the ball quickly to left or right. The ball is tapped forward and backward from left to right with a rolling action of the hands and wrists.

With the standard grip, tap the ball from left to right as you progress down the field, rotating the stick with a half-turn in an anti-clockwise direction as you go. This reverse stick position allows you to contact the ball with the legal hitting face of the stick. Remember that your top hand rotates the stick while your lower hand provides a guide. The head of the stick should remain within a few centimetres of the ball.

Obstacle course

Set up an obstacle course at home or training so you can practise dribbling. First, practise at walking speed, then jogging and eventually at running speed.

The reverse dribble

The **reverse dribble** is used to create space and time when your opponent has blocked your path ahead. Standing with your left foot ahead of your right, the ball is located to the right side of your left foot instep. Now move the ball by turning the stick head around the front of the ball and tapping it backwards sharply.

Skills

Passing the ball to a team-mate

Hockey is a team game so you must be able to pass the ball well. Remember the ABC of passing:

A. Be **Aware** of the positions of your team-mates and opponents;

B. Be **Balanced**; and

C. Have **Control** of the ball.

The drive

Use the **drive** for powering the ball downfield or for goalshooting.

The flick pass

As the **flick pass** lifts the ball into the air, use for a shot at goal, a long **overhead** pass or a short pass over an opponent's lowered stick.

Adopt a push pass grip, and from a side-on position, angle your stick back and under the ball. In a quick action, pull with your left hand and push powerfully with your right to raise the ball.

Drive

From the standard grip, put both hands together at the top of the stick. With the ball to your front and right side, swing back to chest height and step forward so that your left foot is level with the ball.

With straight arms and wrists cocked, contact the ball with the middle of the stick head.

Do not swing higher than shoulder height, on either your backswing or your follow through.

The push pass

While the **push pass** lacks the speed of the drive, its accuracy makes it effective over short distances.

Push pass

The slap hit

The **slap hit** is a similar shot to the push pass, but has a low backswing. With a push pass grip, use this pass for long, powerful passes or split-second slaps at goal.

Adopting the dribble grip, the push pass swing begins from the heel of the front foot.

From a side-on position, transfer your weight smoothly to your front foot.

No backswing is required as the stick is in contact with the ball throughout the motion.

Ball/goal directions

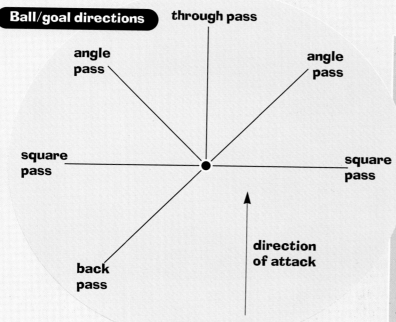

through pass

angle pass

angle pass

square pass

square pass

back pass

direction of attack

The directions the ball can travel in relation to the goal are:
• Square pass, which travels at right-angles to the sideline. Use when attacking players link up to move the ball across the field.
• Through pass, which travels almost parallel to the sideline. Use against two opponents who are standing level with one another.
• Angle pass, which is when the ball travels diagonally to left or right towards the sideline.
• Back pass, which is ideal when faced with a wall of defenders. Use to move play from a congested area to a free space.

Skills

Right-side trap

Keep your eyes focused on the ball.

Receiving the ball

This is the skill of **trapping** the ball with your stick, moving into position and then preparing to shoot, pass or dribble. Usually, you don't need to stop the ball as you will learn to control and then re-position it, ready for your next move. Whether you are trapping a ball approaching from the left or the right, follow these key points:

• Focus your eyes on the ball and move quickly so you are in the path of the approaching ball.

• Lean the top of your stick slightly forward, and allow the stick to give a little as it meets the ball.

• Trap the ball clear of your feet and then move quickly into position to pass, shoot or dribble.

Dodging an opponent

Dodges give your opponent the impression that you are moving in one direction when, in fact, you are moving in another. When your opponent is committed to covering this first move, you then change direction and move past him or her on the other side. Your aim is to wrong-foot your opponent and then accelerate around him or her.

Left dodge

Move to your opponent's left so that he or she gets ready to tackle you from that side.

As you get closer, tap the ball to his or her right and accelerate away quickly.

Right dodge

As you dribble towards your opponent, pretend that you will move to his or her stick side.

Just as you reach your opponent, tap the ball to his or her left and accelerate away quickly.

Skills

Tackling an opponent

The purpose of **tackling** is to gain possession of the ball; force your opponent to pass; or stop your opponent's progress. Remember to watch the ball, not your opponent or his or her stick. You will find the **block tackle** and the **poke tackle** easy to master.

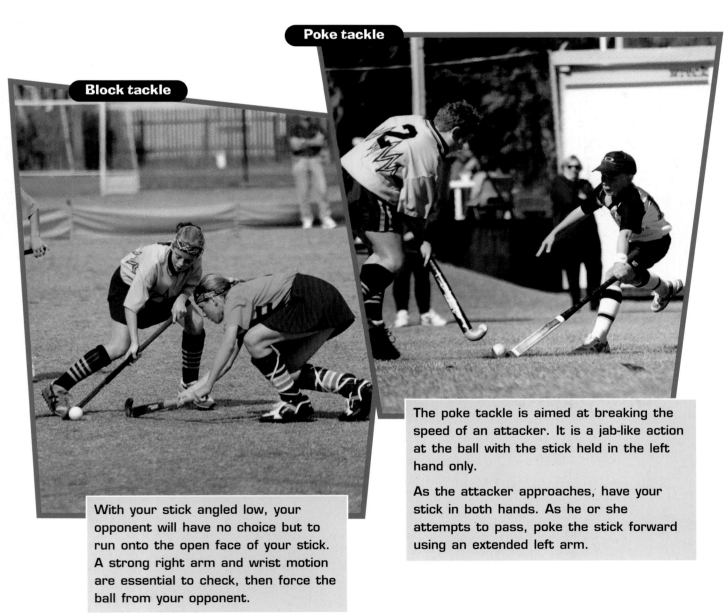

Poke tackle

Block tackle

With your stick angled low, your opponent will have no choice but to run onto the open face of your stick. A strong right arm and wrist motion are essential to check, then force the ball from your opponent.

The poke tackle is aimed at breaking the speed of an attacker. It is a jab-like action at the ball with the stick held in the left hand only.

As the attacker approaches, have your stick in both hands. As he or she attempts to pass, poke the stick forward using an extended left arm.

Shooting goals

Goals win games, and as a team, your aim is to score more goals than your opponent and to concede less goals than you score. These coaching tips may increase your chance of scoring. The basic passing skills of the slap hit, the push pass, the flick pass and the drive must be learned. In each case, plant your front foot close to the ball, keeping ball, stick, foot and head in as close a line as possible.

If the goalkeeper does stop a shoot, move in quickly for the rebound. If he or she is slow to clear the ball, you will be ready to pounce and shoot again.

Shooting goals

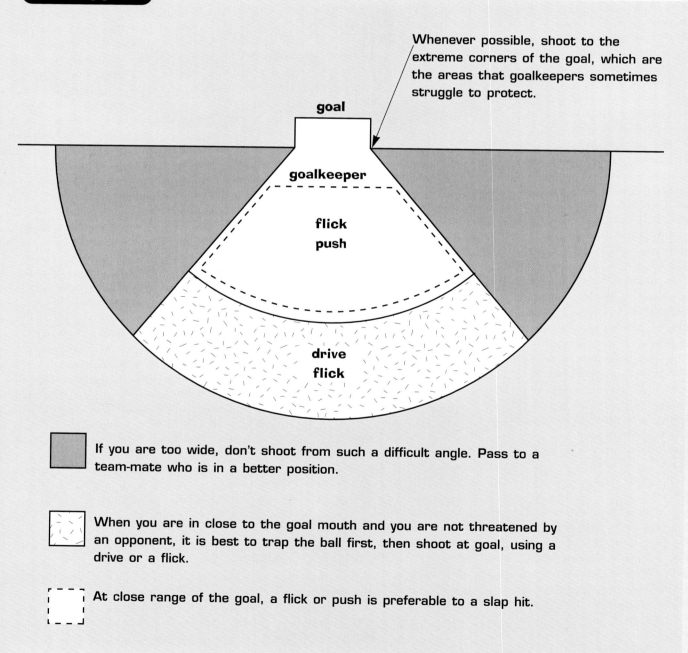

Whenever possible, shoot to the extreme corners of the goal, which are the areas that goalkeepers sometimes struggle to protect.

goal

goalkeeper

flick
push

drive
flick

If you are too wide, don't shoot from such a difficult angle. Pass to a team-mate who is in a better position.

When you are in close to the goal mouth and you are not threatened by an opponent, it is best to trap the ball first, then shoot at goal, using a drive or a flick.

At close range of the goal, a flick or push is preferable to a slap hit.

Skills

Goalkeeping

As goalkeeper, it is your job to stop the ball passing into the goal.

Saving shots

Low shots within reach should be stopped with the pads. The ball should then be pushed or hit wide, towards the sidelines.

When the ball is airborne, you will need to stop it with your stick or hand. Use your hand whenever possible, but when the ball is beyond reach use your stick. As the ball falls to the ground, you must recover instantly to clear the ball, ready to re-position yourself for further saves.

As the ball approaches from the right, move to this side, with your weight on your right foot. For high saves to the left, use your left glove. For waist high saves or below, point your palm slightly downwards. For balls above the waist, point your palms slightly upwards.

Ready stance

As your opponents approach their goal, be prepared for a possible shot by moving into the ready stance. With your feet about shoulder-width apart, knees bent and weight slightly forward, keep your stick in your right hand and your left hand at chest height.

The block save

The block save is a double-leg stop of shots usually hit at goal from around the edge of the goal circle. Used frequently on uneven surfaces, the block is a good technique for shots on goal that are slightly lifted or bouncing.

Shots at goal will come from several angles, and as goalkeeper (GK) you must move into a line directly behind the oncoming ball.

The split save

When the ball is too wide to save in the upright position, use the split save. Remember to warm your groin muscles and hamstrings beforehand.

Drop to the ground in the splits position, with your front leg fully extended and your rear leg tucked up behind in support. To help with a quick recovery, push down hard with your left hand to raise yourself up again.

Covering the angles

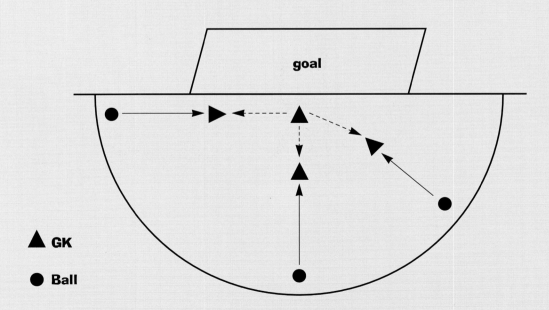

▲ GK

● Ball

This illustration shows an imaginary semi-circle which the goalkeeper moves around.

Getting ready

Warm-up to prevent injuries. Start with a slow jog twice around your playing area. Then, for a distance of about 10 metres, dribble in and out of several witches' hats.

Shoulder stretch
Hold your elbow and pull your arm across to your chest until you feel the stretch. Repeat on the other side.

Calf stretch
Stand with your feet 60 centimetres from a wall. Move your left foot 60 centimetres to the rear, and push the heel down. Hold the stretch for four to six seconds, then switch legs. Repeat three times for each leg.

Seated hamstring stretch
In a seated position with your legs as shown, reach to touch your toes, while pressing your head down toward your knee. Hold for six seconds. Repeat four times for each leg, alternating legs after each stretch.

Thigh stretch
Balance on one foot, bend your knee and bring the heel of the other foot back and up to your buttock. Pull your leg up and hold the stretch for 20 seconds on each leg. Hold a partner for support.

Arm circles (right)
With your feet shoulder-width apart, circle your arms a total of 30 times, 15 in one direction and 15 in the other.

Star jumps (left)
Stand with your feet together with arms by your sides. Jump and land with feet apart and arms outstretched. Jump back to the original position.

Taking it further

Useful addresses

English Hockey Association
Headquarters
National Hockey Stadium
Silbury Boulevard
Milton Keynes
MK9 1HA
Telephone: 01908 544644
Fax: 01908 241106

Great Britain Olympic Hockey Board
78 Gristhorpe Road
Selly Oak
Birmingham
B29 7SW
Tel: 0121 472 2252

Hockey Rules Board
St Audries
26 Stompond Lane
Walton-on-Thames
Surrey
KT12 1HB
Tel: 01932 220962

(The English Hockey Network also has Regional Development Officers throughout the UK.)

Irish Ladies Hockey Union
95 Sandymount Road
Dublin 4
Tel: 353 1 660 6780

Irish Hockey Union (Men)
Ground Floor
6a Woodbine Park
Blackrock
Co Dublin
Tel: 353 1 260 0028
Fax: 353 1 260 0087

Scottish Hockey Union
34 Cramond Road North
Edinburgh
EH4 6JD
Tel: 0131 312 8870
Fax: 0131 312 7829

Welsh Hockey Union
80 Woodville Road
Cathays, Cardiff
CF2 4ED
Tel: 01222 233257
Fax: 01222 233258

Further reading

EHA *Know the Game: Hockey*, A & C Black, London, 1998
Cadman, J. *The Skills of the Game: Hockey*, Crowood Press Wiltshire, 1993
Percival, L. *Hockey Handbook*, Baker & Taylor, 1995

Glossary

block tackle a tackle using the open stick face with both hands on the stick

centre pass used to start play or restart play after a goal is scored

close dribble to dribble with the ball in close contact to the stick

dodge a fast body movement made by the player with the ball

dribbling to run with control of the ball

drive a powerful hit using a full length grip of the stick

flick pass lifting the ball with a severe wrist action

free hit taken by the non-offending team after an infringement

hit-in a pass taken by the non-offending team when the ball crosses over the sideline

Indian dribble a passing technique whereby the player passes the ball and then immediately sprints into space to receive a return pass

obstruction using the body to shield the ball from an opponent

open dribble running with the ball by tapping it a short distance at a time as you run with it

overhead a pass which evades opponents by lofting over their heads

penalty corner awarded when a defender intentionally sends the ball over the goal-line

penalty stroke taken after a goal circle infringement from the penalty spot, which is seven metres in front of goal

poke tackle a jab-like stick action aimed at breaking the speed of an attacker

push pass a pass requiring no backswing

reverse use of the stick on the left-hand side by turning the left hand

reverse dribble used to create space. The ball is tapped backwards.

scanning using vision to assess options while on or off the ball

scoop to raise the ball with a shovelling action

slap hit a method of hitting without changing the dribble grip

tackling methods of gaining possession from your opponent

trapping used to bring a loose or passed ball under control

Index

Hockey
Bernie Blackall

First published in Great Britain by Heinemann Library, Halley Court, Jordan Hill,
Oxford OX2 8EJ, a division of Reed Educational and Professional Publishing Ltd.
Heinemann is a registered trademark of Reed Educational & Professional Publishing Limited.

The moral right of the proprietor has been asserted.

04 03 02 01 00
10 9 8 7 6 5 4 3 2 1

OXFORD MELBOURNE AUCKLAND
JOHANNESBURG BLANTYRE GABORONE
IBADAN PORTSMOUTH NH (USA) CHICAGO

Series cover and text design by Karen Young
Cover by Smarty-pants Design
Paged by Jo Pritchard
Edited by Sarah Russell
Illustrations by Joy Antonie
Picture research by Lara Artis
Production by Ruth Slattery
Film separations by Typescan, Adelaide
Printed in Hong Kong by Wing King Tong

British Library Cataloguing in Publication Data
Blackall, Bernie
Hockey. – (Top Sport)
1.Hockey – Juvenile literature
I.Title
796.3'55

ISBN 0 431 08512 9

This title is also available in a hardback library edition (ISBN 0 431 08508 0).

Acknowledgements
The Publishers would like to thank the following for permission to reproduce photographs:
Bernie Blackall: cover (right), pp 14, 17, 26. Coo-ee Historical Picture Library: p 9. Empics Ltd/
Tony Marshall: pp 6, 7. Sue and Wies Fajzullin Photography: cover (left), pp 4, 5, 11, 15, 18, 22, 24.
Barry Silkstone: p 13. Sporting Pix/Bob Thomas: p 8.

Our thanks to Brian Ingleby, Dartmouth Community College,
for his assistance in the preparation of this book.

Every effort has been made to contact copyright holders of any material reproduced in this book.
Any omissions will be rectified in subsequent printings if notice is given to the Publisher.

Any words appearing in the text in bold, **like this**, are explained in the Glossary.